FAULTLESS GRAMMAR

The busy lawyer's reminder guide

By Ben Staveley

© Ben Staveley 2017
Illustrations © Patrick Blower 2017
ISBN: 978-1-9997452-0-2

Published by Ben Staveley
34 Oxford Road
Putney
London SW15 2LQ

ben@thestaveleys.com

www.benstaveley.co.uk

Please read me

This guide has to beg for readers. Most people at whom it is aimed would instinctively shun a guide to grammar and punctuation as beneath their dignity.

These opening paragraphs try to persuade you to swallow your pride and read further.

Clients judge lawyers by their writing

All lawyers know that they need to write well professionally. Here are four obvious reasons:

- lawyers spend much of their time drafting documents for deals and cases, and writing to clients and others. Written words are a big part of a lawyer's primary output

- clients cannot usually evaluate lawyers' technical ability, which they take for granted. But they **can** tell how easily they can understand what their lawyer has written for them

- lawyers are meant to be meticulous. So if clients spot errors in their lawyers' English, they worry that the lawyers may be too careless to have looked at the law properly either

- however many good meals you have eaten there, it only takes one bad experience to turn you against a restaurant. In the same way, one writing slip can cause disproportionate harm to a lawyer's reputation. That goes for the reputation of a lawyer within a firm, just as much as (and in fact because) it also goes for a firm's reputation with its client

If all this is right, it must make sense to go the extra mile to insulate your writing from any possible criticism.

A philosophical justification for respecting 'the rules'

But, you may object, does any of this really justify a grammar and punctuation guide? Isn't such a work more suitable for a schoolchild than for someone who is already at a professional level?

This guide isn't written by a 'prescriptivist' stickler who relishes catching people out and rails against the language's decline from a supposed Golden Age. The 'rules' of English grammar aren't owned by sticklers, whatever they may like to believe. The rules reflect how everyone uses the English language. That language is constantly evolving, which means the rules are, too.

But all readers – sticklers or otherwise – like to read writing that conveys its message smoothly, preferably at first reading. They resent the jolt that an ungrammatical sentence gives them. The jolt arises because the writer has not followed the conventions that have grown up to reflect how most users of English express themselves when trying to say or write something clearly (which is all that 'grammar' amounts to).

Punctuation, around which a similar body of consistent practice has grown up, shares most of these same characteristics.

It follows that in talking about 'correct' and 'incorrect' usage, of 'rules' which are 'observed' or 'breached', we are not trying to stand Canute-like against the tide of the development of the English language. Rather, we are realists, concentrating our efforts on avoiding **how** we write distracting our reader from understanding **what** we are trying to convey.

A reader who recognises that a writer has 'got something wrong' has two reactions

A 'jolted' reader may have to read the rogue sentence again to work out what the writer really meant. At best, the process of absorbing information is slowed or interrupted. This is bad enough. But it becomes even worse if a busy reader (and what other type is there?) abandons, in exasperation, the task of trying to work out what the writer was trying to get across.

Sophisticated readers who notice breaches of the rules rapidly lose faith, mentally categorising the guilty writer as ignorant (they didn't know about the convention in question) or inconsiderate (they knew about it, but decided to go ahead anyway). Neither stigma is one that most writers will want to attract.

From confident to faultless

This guide tries to give you the tools to reduce to vanishing point the chances that you will write something that, because of the way it is written, will make your reader think the less of you.

Two bits of news may encourage you.

First, this guide is based on a wide survey of the writing of lawyers entering the profession. So it can confidently claim to cover all the most common problems.

Second, the guide can be quite short. This is because, though some hapless writers ingeniously find new elephant traps to stumble into, most errors lie within a narrow set of categories.

To put it another way, if you master all the things in this guide, you are likely to have all you need to move from a confident to a **faultless** writer.

And most of what follows you will know already.

A colourful note to end with

The colour code is that correct examples are shown in blue, incorrect usage in red. If the examples are in ordinary black type, they are neither clearly right nor clearly wrong.

Contents

Grammar

Number difficulties: singular and plural

A verb should agree with its subject

Many languages 'inflect' more than English. This means that speakers vary the ends of words to reflect number, gender or case (subject or object case, for example). Je parle, tu parles, il/elle parle. Nous parlons, vous parlez, ils/elles parlent.

English regular verbs normally inflect only by adding an 's' to the third person singular (I, you, we and they *write*, but he/she *writes*). *Be*, with its various present tense forms *am/are/is*, is unusual.

It is a basic rule of the grammar of any language to inflect a verb accurately – to use the form that goes with the subject so that the subject and verb 'agree'. And because English verbs inflect so simply, writers have very little excuse for getting it wrong. If a writer does blunder, a reader reacts badly: it seems careless.

Blunders are nonetheless common. Often, the trigger is that the subject is plural, but is made up of two elements linked by *and* – but the writer still chooses a singular form of the verb. What seems to happen is that the writer has forgotten, by the time he or she arrives at the verb, that the subject is plural – particularly if the latter component is longer than the first, which ends up being disregarded:

> The weakness of sterling and the likelihood that it will weaken still further in the medium term *makes* it more critical that the trade deficit is addressed (should be *make*)

The reverse problem arises if the subject is truly singular, but ends with a noun that is itself plural:

> The need to reach out to people from many different backgrounds, of different attainments and with different interests, *are* a formidable difficulty (should be *is*)

But you do get special cases where the 'obvious' answer is wrong or doubtful

Careful writers need to understand the boundaries of the principle. Consider the sentence:

Fish and chips *are* my favourite meal

Most readers feel this is wrong (and would prefer *is*), because the two are regarded as a single menu item.

And sometimes the same noun can sensibly be regarded as either singular or plural, depending on the context. All of these next examples will strike most readers as correct:

Gymnastics *was* my favourite activity during PE

The mental gymnastics required to keep up with the lecture *were* seriously tiring

Politics *is* a rough old game

His politics *are* somewhere to the right of Genghis Khan

Two plus two *is* four

Two and two *make* four

And care is needed with linkages other than a simple *and*:

> The price of alcohol, if taken together with the controls on selling it, *makes* it inaccessible to most children (better than *make*)

An *or* formation linking two singulars takes a singular verb:

> A partner or an associate *has* to check the trainee's drafting

But if the latter term after *or* is itself plural, the choice is harder. You might see:

> The Prime Minister or the Cabinet members has to take responsibility for the decision

or perhaps:

> The Prime Minister or the Cabinet members have to take responsibility for the decision

Traditional grammar books favour the second, but it's not an easy choice.

Every, each, either, neither, any *and* none

Some of these are easier to handle than the others.

Every always takes the singular:

> Every soldier *was* ready at 6 o'clock sharp

Each also takes the singular:

> Each child *has* brought a packed lunch

But the position of *each* can make the plural preferable to most readers:

> The boys each *want* to go if there are enough tickets

Either and *neither* are also usually singular:

> Either the doctor or the anaesthetist **has** to take the lion's share of the blame for the incident

> Neither of the pandas **was** interested in breeding

But if the two elements to which *either* or *neither* refers are themselves plural, the verb is itself plural:

> Neither the Montagues nor the Capulets **were** averse to a good fight

Any is normally singular:

> Any of these arguments **is** surely strong enough to convince the judge

But *any* can also appear, quite naturally, with a plural verb:

> I don't think any of the crowd **have** shelter from the rain if it arrives

Here the context is that the writer is thinking of some proportion of a crowd attending an outdoor event of some kind, and is thinking of whether a subset of that crowd, itself numbering many people, will have shelter from the rain. To illustrate the point, if you asked X the question, 'Will any of the crowd have shelter from the rain if it arrives?' and X said, 'Yes', you might think X's answer a little odd if it emerged that the only reason for the answer was that one member of the crowd, and one alone, would stay dry.

Sticklers see *none* as singular (the equivalent of *not one*):

None of the trainees **is** available to work on the document this evening

But a plural use is certainly possible, as in this example:

All the trainees claim to have completed the module, but almost none of them **have** completed the feedback form

Some nouns can take the singular or the plural

Some nouns, particularly denoting groups of people, are sometimes seen with singular or plural. Usually, the singular is seen as the 'correct' or formal use, so if the ambition is to keep sticklers happy, it is better to stick with it. For example:

The company **is** under a duty to file its accounts by March 31

Sticklers who insist on this are right in the sense that *company* is an obvious singular (compare *companies*). Sticklers with legal knowledge will also point out that a company has its own legal personality, separate from its members. But they would also prefer a singular, even if the particular entity does not have that characteristic:

The partnership **is** united on the best course of action

However, in modern English, many speakers and writers would naturally use the plural with a subject that is technically a singular noun (and the use of a plural 'their' does not seem incongruous):

England **have** to score 247 to beat the Australians

The crowd **were** craning **their** necks to see whether the ref had shown the goalkeeper a red card

The plural tends to be more readily accepted where, as in the second of these two examples, the focus is on what each particular member of the group is doing – there is in effect a suppressed *each* in the sentence. In the first example, that focus is lacking – it's not that *each* member of the England team needs to make 247, they just need to get that total between them. So the plural is more marginal, and indeed would be resisted by many readers. British readers are more readily accepting of the plural than US ones.

In a legal context, it may be safer to avoid offending anyone who cares about this point by adhering to the singular where the noun is formally singular. Thus, while

The board **have** to take individual responsibility for the prospectus

and

The other side **need** to come back to us with a clearer idea of **their** concerns are both defensible in ordinary speech (hence appear in blue), a writer who is not aiming for a deliberately informal style may be safer with a singular:

> Each board member **has** to take individual responsibility for the prospectus

and

> The other side **needs** to come back to us with a clearer idea of **its** concerns

Their *as a singular to avoid an accusation of sexism*

English lacks a gender-neutral pronoun for human beings in the third person singular. We have only *he* or *she* (subject) and *him* or *her* (object). We also have 'it', of course, but not, otherwise than very insultingly, for a person.

Old-fashioned writers were happy simply to assume that *he* or *him* would do to refer to an imaginary representative person, but modern writers with any sensitivity are alert to the possibility that readers will react against the practice. Alternatives, though, are hard to like. Going for *she* and *her* consistently instead seems equally discriminatory; alternating

between *he* and *him* in one chapter, and *she* and *her* in the next, artificial and confusing; using *he/she* (or *(s)he*) and *him/her* merely laborious. Some enthusiasts have busied themselves devising a new pronoun. But history suggests that they will have their work cut out to get it accepted, even if they can first agree on what it should be.

Sensitivity to transgender politics makes the problem more urgent, but no easier to solve. Does *he* or *she* in itself make unwarranted assumptions?

Out of these difficulties, another idea has emerged. The *he* versus *she* disparity does not arise in the plural, where we have only gender-neutral *they* or *them*. So writers often choose to go with the plural instead:

> The best way of retaining the confidence of a patient is to listen to their problems carefully before prescribing them any medication

But in a simple case, it still jars with some readers:

> A trainee should do ***their*** own research

would seem too obvious a breach of singular/plural consistency to be acceptable to some sticklers, who are more offended by the number shift than they would be with any of the alternatives. Singular *their* continues to gain ground, and may end up becoming generally acceptable; but at present, the writer who uses it needs to recognise it as a risk. (Some readers may have bridled when they came across it on page 8.) The best advice at present may be to avoid the sticklers' wrath by recasting the sentence fully into the plural:

> The best way of retaining the confidence of ***patients*** is to listen to ***their*** problems carefully before prescribing ***them*** any medication

> ***Trainees*** should do ***their*** own research

Case difficulties: subjects, objects and possessives

The three cases

English grammar requires inflection for different cases. The term 'case' here is used in a grammatical sense to denote the particular role a noun or pronoun plays in the sentence, and is most easily seen (if you are unfamiliar with the concept) by the ungrammaticality of examples like *me went to the theatre*; *I told he not to do it*; *she went to fetch she coat.*

The correct versions illustrate the three most common cases:

I went to the theatre

I is the subject form of the first person singular pronoun, not *me*. *I* is the appropriate form of the pronoun because the pronoun is the subject of the verb *went*: *I* did the action of the verb. The subject case is also called the **nominative** case.

I told **him** not to do it

Him is the object form of the masculine third person singular pronoun, not *he*. *Him* is the appropriate form because the pronoun is the (indirect) object of the verb *told*: the subject is *I*. The object case is also called the **accusative** case.

She went to fetch **her** coat

Her is the possessive form of the feminine third person pronoun, not *she*. The possessive form is demanded because the role of *her* in the sentence is to denote that the coat belonged to person to whom *her* refers. The possessive case is also called the **genitive** case.

This shows that for **pronouns**, we have inflection across three cases. But **nouns** have the same form for subject/nominative as for object/accusative:

The ***horse*** bolted from the stable

The groom finally tracked down the ***horse***

Only with the possessive/genitive form do we see any inflection:

The ***horse's*** owner paid for the damage it had caused when it escaped

Errors with the possessive are mostly associated with botching the apostrophe, one of whose major roles is in the possessive case. So they are dealt with later, both for nouns and pronouns.

It remains to deal here with confusion as between the subject and object form of pronouns. Getting it right is reasonably straightforward, but some writers still find ways to get it wrong and so offend their readers.

Handling subject and object forms of pronouns: I, me etc

Most writers of English do not have to think to get the case right as between *I* and *me*; *we* and *us*; *he* and *him*; *she* and *her*; and *they* and *them*. They use the right form wholly unconsciously.

But some writers get misled by extrapolating what happens in ordinary speech. If a colleague asks you *Who is attending the 4 pm meeting?* you might easily respond by saying *Helen and me* rather than *Helen and I*. But *Helen and I* is strictly correct, since your reply is short for *Helen and I [are attending the meeting]*. *Helen* and *I* are both in the subject case because both are subjects of the unexpressed verb *are*. Few speakers would say

Helen and me are attending without knowing that they are being ungrammatical; and they wouldn't dream of writing it.

From that starting point, speakers develop an illusory fear that they must somehow be falling short of the required standard of formality if they **ever** use *me*. This leads them to overreact by using *I* even where *me* is called for, and they write, incorrectly:

The meeting will be attended by Helen and *I*

Here *I* is wrong, as is easily shown if Helen is not going:

The meeting will be attended by *I*

is obviously wrong.

The same issue arises, perhaps rather more rarely, in the plural:

If the package arrives, please inform *we* and the company secretary immediately (should be *us*)

or in the third person:

He hoped to receive an invitation for *he* and his girlfriend to attend Wimbledon (should be *him*)

Again, the error is easily identified if the pronoun is considered in isolation:

If the package arrives, please inform *we* immediately

He hoped to receive an invitation for *he* to attend Wimbledon

But in some cases (usually involving the verb *be*, which is strictly followed by the subject case), either subject or object case may be acceptable, usually with the subject case representing the more formal version:

It's *I* they voted for

It's *me* they voted for

Myself *not a good solution*

The me-phobia that causes *The meeting will be attended by Helen and I* also triggers another stratagem to avoid a simple *me* in case it might be wrong – resorting to the reflexive form of the pronoun:

> The meeting will be attended by Helen and *myself*

or, even if Helen's not going:

> The meeting will be attended by *myself*

It may not just be nervousness about the correct form of the personal pronoun that causes this. After all, a salesperson, eager to appear super-polite, will sometimes ask

> Can I get anything for *yourself* at all?

when the non-reflexive form of the pronoun, whether in subject or object case, can only be *you*.

The reflexive form *yourself* in sentences like this emphasises the salesperson's deference to the customer, which may well be the (subconscious) reason for using it. But in the *myself* examples, the speaker or writer risks coming across as more self-important, and that's an unattractive impression to give. The reader doesn't detect self-importance when *myself* is used in its normal reflexive sense, as in *I've made myself a diary note so I don't miss the meeting*. So it is better, stylistically, to restrict it to that role, and otherwise stick to the simple pronoun:

> The meeting will be attended by Helen and me

Who *and* whom

Whom is the object/accusative form of *who*. So all the following sentence fragments are correct:

> The newsreader *who* forgot to read the Autocue (subject case)

> The newsreader *whom* the station fired (object case – direct object)

> The newsreader to *whom* several messages of commiseration were sent (object case – indirect object)

Sticklers are vigilant about the distinction between *who* and *whom*. Most speakers and writers naturally observe the distinction and use *whom* for the object form, especially when the word is preceded by a preposition. The third example above sounds like an owl if *who* appears incorrectly:

> The newsreader to *who* several messages of commiseration were sent

So *whom* is not about to disappear from the language.

In informal spoken English, *who* occurs quite often where *whom* is strictly correct, especially where it appears at the front of the clause it introduces, which disguises its grammatical function:

> *Who* do you want to talk to?

The latitude afforded by listeners to speakers, however, is greater than that afforded by readers to writers, and many readers will think the less of you if you write:

> Can I enquire *who* you have asked to represent the firm at the conference?

Here *who* is in fact the object of *asked*, but is in the classic subject position at the head of a clause.

The *who* in this example is also arguably right if the sentence is regarded as shorthand for

> Can I enquire *who* [is the person] you have asked to represent the firm at the conference?

when *who* is in fact in subject case. But a stickler may not realise this, and a writer does not in any event have the chance to defend himself (herself? themselves?) The safer course is to write the version that is grammatically unimpeachable and thus stickler-resistant:

> Can I enquire *whom* you have asked to represent the firm at the conference?

Coordinations: not only...but also, *and similar constructions*

Grammar problems often bedevil unconfident writers when they try to use **coordinations**. This is the grammatical term for the relationship of two or more parts of a sentence joined by expressions like *either...or, neither...nor*, and *both...and*. But another coordination gives rise to what is perhaps the most common error of all: *not only...but also*.

Here's what an error looks like:

> The company had filed ***not only*** its accounts for the previous year ***but also*** sent in its management accounts for each quarter

The grammatical rule that is breached here is that both limbs of the coordination – first, the part following *not only* down to *but also*, and second, the part following *but also* – must be parallel constructions which follow on from the words that precede the *not only*.

Here, if we look at what follows *not only*, we have *its accounts for the previous year*. This works fine with the language that precedes *not only* – *The company had filed... its accounts for the previous year* makes perfect sense.

So far so good; but when we look at what follows *but also* and add it to what precedes *not only* we have *The company had filed...sent in its management accounts for each quarter*. The two verbs are in a train crash and the sentence doesn't work. It needs to be:

> The company had ***not only*** filed its accounts for the previous year ***but also*** sent in its management accounts for each quarter

Another example:

> The chairman needs to be *either* a master of tact *or* face the rebellion head on

Here the coordination is *either...or* and the second half of the sentence stumbles: *The chairman needs to be... face the rebellion head on.* A better sentence would be:

> The chairman needs *either* to be a master of tact *or* to face the rebellion head on

And here's another:

> The case involved *both* a claim in tort *and* in contract

The coordination is *both...and,* and the sentence needs to be recast as

> The case involved *both* a claim in tort *and* a claim in contract

or perhaps

> The case involved claims in *both* tort *and* contract

Split infinitives

Some sticklers take a delight in finding a split infinitive and, when they do, pursing their lips in disapproval. Most serious grammarians, though, don't do any such thing. They think that there is in fact nothing to disapprove of. In their view, the supposed rule is in truth merely a superstition based on an assumed parallel between English and Latin.

The supposed error occurs when a word, usually an adverb, is inserted in the infinitive form of the verb, which is the form with *to* preceding it – the version Tennyson uses in the last line of his great poem *Ulysses*:

> *to* strive, *to* seek, *to* find, and not *to* yield

The sticklers object therefore to something like:

> The secretary tried to faithfully record the course of the debate

And of course they would not like *to boldly go* anywhere, let alone, along-side Captain Kirk, *where no man has gone before.*

The sticklers would automatically 'correct'

The secretary tried to faithfully record the course of the debate

to

The secretary tried **faithfully to record** the course of the debate

or

The secretary tried **to record faithfully** the course of the debate

However, if the stickler goes for the former 'fix', the meaning may subtly have changed. In the original *tried to faithfully record*, it is fairly clear that the adverb *faithfully* qualifies *to record*: the secretary was trying to make sure his notes were a faithful representation of the debate. With the *tried faithfully to record* version, the *faithfully* attaches itself to *tried*, giving a slightly different nuance.

With a little ingenuity, you can come up with cases where unsplitting a split infinitive changes the meaning of the sentence more radically:

The Cabinet decided **to immediately commission** a new runway

is a breach of the supposed rule. But if you 'correct' it to

The Cabinet decided **immediately to commission** a new runway

you change the meaning: the sense becomes that the decision was taken straight away, rather than that the decision was for prompt action.

So a writer needs to tread carefully here. But as a working rule, it may make sense to try to avoid splitting infinitives. After all, the purpose of writing is to communicate, and you can't do that easily if your reader is distracted, even if the distraction is for a bizarre reason you don't agree with.

TO CONCLUSIVELY SPLIT THE INFINITIVE

LAB

31

Beginning a sentence with a conjunction

Some nervous writers, based on a rule they were taught when they were ten years old, believe that they will be committing some error if they ever begin a sentence with a word like *and, but* or *so*.

So this sentence is faulty because it begins with *so*. And this one too, because it starts with *and*. But (three in a row) there is in truth no such rule. (But the technique becomes noticeable if it is overused. So it is best used more sparingly than in this paragraph.)

Many great writers have begun sentences with an *and* or a *but* without harming their reputations in the slightest. You would be unlikely to offend any reader by doing so. Indeed, if it helps you shorten the average length of your sentences, it may improve your writing style, not harm it. Readers absorb short sentences more easily than longer ones, and are grateful if writers are considerate enough to keep sentences short.

One time that a writer should be wary of beginning a sentence with a conjunction is if trying to adopt a particularly **formal** style of writing. As you will see if you re-read the second paragraph of this section, starting sentences with a conjunction can come across as breezy in tone. If you are trying to write a formal piece of advice, you should consider whether you have achieved the right impression with this technique (and you might also decide to avoid contractions such as *don't, couldn't, should've*, and use the uncontracted forms).

Hanging participles

The hanging participle error is one which does not enrage readers so much as cause their lips to curl with amusement – because the writer often creates an unintentionally comic effect.

Before an explanation, here are some examples:

Swooping just above the promenade, the mayor nearly collided with a seagull

With half an eye on the bookmakers' odds, the thoroughbred paraded before the eager crowd

Internationally renowned and with expertise in every possible area of the law, I can as a student think of nowhere I would rather work than this firm

The reason that these sentences strike an unconsciously comic effect is that a reader naturally expects the initial phrase to be associated with the **subject** of the sentence. The subjects, in these sentences, here occupy their usual position at the front of the main part of the sentence, immediately following the initial phrase: *the mayor, the thoroughbred* and *I*. But the writer wasn't trying to refer to the subject: the phrases were meant to refer to *the seagull, the crowd* and *this firm*. The humour arises as the reader resolves the temporary miscue. But miscues cost time, readers are busy, and writers owe it to them to avoid the delay of a frustrated expectation, even if it causes a smile. A sophisticated reader will lose a little faith in the writer every time something like this happens, and would prefer the sentences to be recast in a way that avoids the misassociation:

The mayor nearly collided with a seagull *that was swooping just above the promenade*

The thoroughbred paraded before the eager crowd, *who kept half an eye on the bookmakers' odds*

I can as a student think of nowhere I would rather work than this firm, *which is internationally renowned and has expertise in every possible area of the law*

Punctuation

Punctuation helps a reader follow a writer's train of thought. Unlike speakers, writers can't use pauses, or vary their tone of voice, to help convey their meaning. They can, however, use punctuation to achieve a similar effect.

Just as a speaker who gabbles or makes no concessions to a listener comes across as rude, so also does a writer who does not take the trouble to punctuate accurately. This means that a careful writer has to know the various conventions that have grown up about how writing should be punctuated.

As with their grammar, lawyers are vulnerable to losing the respect of their readers if they get their punctuation wrong. Clients want their lawyers to be painstaking and fastidious in their advice. Leaving a punctuation mark out when it is needed, or putting one in the wrong place, comes across as slipshod.

This guide should answer most questions that you have. As with the section dealing with grammar, most of it will be familiar to most readers.

Apostrophes

As a lawyer, ignore them at your peril

Many writers today allow themselves to ignore apostrophes in informal style, for example in messaging their friends. But when writing formally – and for a lawyer, that means in pretty much every piece of professional writing – a writer should be careful to use apostrophes accurately.

Fortunately, the apostrophe rules are few in number, and – in modern English usage – reasonably clear. Only at the margins are they doubtful. The sting in the tail is that a misused apostrophe is wince-inducingly obvious to a sophisticated reader. Nor should you think that it's OK to leave apostrophes out on the basis they're unnecessary. Again, educated readers will see this as unacceptable.

The apostrophe has two distinct uses

First, it signifies **omission** – that something in the writing has been left out.

Second, it indicates **possession** – that something belongs to somebody,

or something, else.

These two distinct uses are dealt with in turn below.

Apostrophes signalling omission

These are most often found in contractions, especially where the full version contains *not* – for example *can't, shouldn't, won't* (short for *cannot, should not, will not*). Modern English doesn't allow more than one apostrophe in a single word, so even though *shan't* is short for *shall not* it's not these days written as *sha'n't* – though once upon a time, the double apostrophe was regarded as correct.

Other examples of contractions:

There's a breathless hush in the close tonight (contracted word: *is*)

She's done all the necessary research (*has*)

They've answered our questions in that email (*have*)

I'll send it later (*will* or *shall*)

As already noted, contractions are themselves more informal in style than the full 'uncontracted' versions. They allow a writer to get closer to the rhythms of ordinary speech, and speaking is often a more informal form of communication than writing. Lawyers need to ask themselves whether, in any particular piece of writing, their readers want or expect the informality of style that contractions lend to writing.

Possessive apostrophes

As this guide has already pointed out (see **Case difficulties** above), nouns in English do not 'inflect' (vary) much to indicate the role any particular noun plays in a sentence. But when a noun is being used in a possessive sense, there is some inflection, in which the apostrophe plays an important role.

The rules are few in number, and are not difficult to master, which is why a failure to observe them pains most readers.

Rule 1: the simple case is where a singular noun is used possessively – the possessive form involves adding an 's', and an apostrophe which goes before the 's':

> The *lawyer's* computer had not been switched off

This remains the case if the non-possessive form of the noun ends in 's' already:

> The *class's* attention was diverted by what was happening just outside the window

Rule 2: where a plural ending with an 's' is used possessively, the apostrophe comes after the 's'.

The default rule for how English nouns form plurals is that they add an 's': singular *dog* has plural form *dogs*. Sometimes there is a spelling change going beyond the 's': for example, singular *company* has plural *companies*, and singular *potato* has plural *potatoes*.

In all these cases, the possessive form of the plural noun has an apostrophe after the 's':

> The *dogs'* kennels were ranged against the fence at the back of the compound

> The *potatoes'* skins were not all the same colour as one another

Rule 3: where the plural form does not end in an 's', apply Rule 1: the apostrophe comes before the 's' that is needed to signify that the word is being used in a possessive sense:

> The *children's* lunchboxes were sitting on the table in the hall

The *mice's* tails were surprisingly inconsistent in how quickly they grew

Rule 4: there is a special rule for *it*.

Some otherwise confident writers experience a special kind of torture: they know that there is a special rule distinguishing *its* and *it's* , but can't remember what it is. It's this: where *it's* is a contraction of it is, as at the beginning of this sentence, an apostrophe is needed. But where *its* is merely a possessive, no apostrophe should appear:

Tipperary is known for *its* archaeological heritage

but

It's a long way to Tipperary

Rule 5: with proper names ending in 's', you will see a fair amount of variation – sometimes a conventional apostrophe plus an 's', and sometimes just an apostrophe. The safest course here is to write the word as it is spoken:

Bridget *Jones's* diary (most speakers would sound the extra 's')

Socrates' draught of hemlock (very few speakers would actually say *Socrates's*)

The cases where the extra 's' is omitted tend to be longer names.

Common apostrophe blunders

Don't be tempted to add an apostrophe to simple plurals (the so-called 'greengrocer's apostrophe' because of the supposed habit of greengrocers of advertising their produce as *cabbage's, cauliflower's* and the like).

Some sticklers object to the apostrophe sometimes found when referring to a decade, as in:

the oil shock of the *1970's*

or with a letter

my sister got ten *A's* in her *GCSE's*

The sticklers have a point: these apostrophes are in one sense merely the greengrocer's apostrophe in another guise. You can argue that an apostrophe here is defensible, but if your main objective is to avoid offending anyone, you are probably safer to leave it out.

But you should include an apostrophe where some figures have been left out – it is then a respectable apostrophe of omission:

the financial crash of *'07/'08*

A trickier task is to distinguish between the possessive and merely 'attributive' (descriptive but not possessive) uses of a name which ends in an 's'. This, for example, is wrong:

The *Linklaters'* lawyers on the other side all seem to work very long hours

The apostrophe suggests a possessive, but here *Linklaters* is simply being used attributively, not as a possessive. It's easy to see this if you think about a name that doesn't end in 's'. Nobody would say or write:

The *Norton Rose's* lawyers arrived at 6 o'clock

Instead you'd naturally go for:

The *Norton Rose* lawyers arrived at 6 o'clock

On the other hand, when the name appears as an adjective without the definite article *the*, it is being used possessively and an apostrophe is called for:

Freshfields' senior partner spoke at the Paris conference

So we have:

a *Moses* basket

but

Moses' tablets of stone

Other mistakes that strike readers as slipshod involve pronouns, which generally do not take an apostrophe:

The other side have their arguments, and we have *our's* (should be *ours*)

Elaine insists the PC is *her's* (should be *hers*)

And *who's* and *whose* are both possible, but have distinct meanings:

Whose is the red Toyota parked in the driveway? (to whom does it belong?)

Who's driving? *Who's* got the keys? (apostrophes of omission, the contractions being short for *who is* and *who has* respectively)

Commas

The simplest marks of all, and able to be used flexibly

As everyone knows, commas are there to help readers make sense of the flow of a sentence – they indicate to a reader that it is time to rest, however briefly, before reading on.

Writers vary in how much they use commas. Lots of commas indicate a 'closed' style, which comes across, to many readers, as a little halting, perhaps even old-fashioned, as in this sentence. Commas are more sparsely used in a more 'open' style that many modern readers find more appealing and modern, as for example in this sentence.

Some lawyers inexcusably draft contract language without any commas at all, which makes the contracts all but unintelligible.

But though writers can legitimately choose between a closed and an open style, comma use is not a free-for-all. Writers still have to obey some rules if they are not to lose readers' faith.

Comma error 1: avoid the comma splice

A comma splice is regarded by sophisticated readers as a breach of the rules. Here is a sentence exhibiting a comma splice:

The company is in difficulty, the finance director has resigned

A comma splice involves a writer constructing one sentence out of two parts, each of which could stand as a separate sentence, and separating them merely with a comma. This is regarded as **wrong**. The above could of course have been written unimpeachably as two sentences:

The company is in difficulty. The finance director has resigned

But writing the two halves as a single sentence, separated by a comma, is a comma splice and needs to be cured.

The diagnosis in itself has provided one cure: simply rewrite the single sentence as two, separated by a full stop.

Three other easy cures are available (it is perhaps because comma splices are so easy to fix that readers look down so strongly on writers who blunder into them).

The first cure is to use a semicolon rather than a comma:

The company is in difficulty; the finance director has resigned

The second cure is to leave the comma, but add a conjunction after it:

The company is in difficulty, **and** the finance director has resigned

But it's not every conjunction that works if you choose this second solution. A list of those that do work is: *for, and, but, yet, or, while, so, nor.*

Longer conjunctions do not work, though. This is still a comma splice:

> The company is in difficulty, **however** the banks are continuing to support it

Finally, the third cure is to use the conjunction without a comma:

> The company is in difficulty **and** the finance director has resigned

This is entirely acceptable, and indeed its 'open' style may appeal to modern readers more than the version with the comma.

It is only with a two-part sentence that the comma splice rule operates. A sentence with three or more components rather than two can be divided by commas, although a conjunction is needed between the last two:

> The company was in difficulty, the finance director resigned **and** the auditors qualified their audit report.

This is just like a list within a sentence:

> The insolvency report was issued to the shareholders, creditors **and** regulators of the company

Comma error 2: do not insert a comma between subject and verb; use 'fencing commas' only in pairs

Commas between a subject and a verb are regarded by modern readers as ugly. Once, though, they were acceptable. Here is Jane Austen in *Northanger Abbey:*

> The progress of Catherine's address from the events of the evening, was as follows.

No sentence from a stylist like Jane Austen can realistically appear in red, but modern writers let themselves down if they do something like this, because most readers would disapprove.

Perhaps some writers find it hard to recognise this error, because a comma can legitimately appear before a verb:

> Elaine, who had previously appeared only in minor roles, shot to prominence as Nora in Ibsen's *A Doll's House* at the National

Here the comma before the verb 'shot' is fine. But that is because its role is one of a pair of 'fencing commas' (also sometimes called 'delimiting commas' or 'bracketing commas') enclosing the subordinate clause *who had previously appeared only in minor roles*. The comma's function here is not to create a pause between subject and verb, but to signify the boundaries of the subordinate clause through which the reader has to pass before the main flow of the sentence is resumed.

Fencing commas are optional where the subordinate clause is short. A writer who favours an open style may choose to write, with no fencing commas:

> My overriding feeling based on my research is that I would enjoy a legal career

Another writer, who prefers a more closed style, or wants to emphasise the importance of the research, may prefer to use fencing commas:

> My overriding feeling, based on my research, is that I would enjoy a legal career

Or, to take an example from earlier in the guide, you might see this:

> The price of alcohol, if taken together with the controls on selling it, makes it inaccessible to most children

But if they appear at all, fencing commas must appear only in pairs. Readers are confused if they appear singly. Some writers exhibit poor control by leaving one out, as in:

> My overriding feeling, based on my research is that I would enjoy a legal career

> My overriding feeling based on my research, is that I would enjoy a legal career

Perhaps – at the risk of overlabouring the point – the best way of curing this problem is to visualise fencing commas as a simpler form of

brackets, which can easily (like this) be used to close off a subordinate part of the sentence. That fits with commas of this type sometimes being called 'bracketing commas'. Pretty much everyone knows that an opening bracket can't exist happily on its own: it needs a closing bracket at the end of whatever it is that needs to be shown as subordinate. So too with fencing commas: one of them is simply one too few.

The 'Oxford comma' explained

Many people have heard vaguely about something called an 'Oxford comma' without necessarily knowing what it is. In case you're interested in an explanation, here it is.

Conventionally, in a list of three or more items contained within a sentence, a comma is compulsory between the earlier items on the list, but can be omitted between the last two:

The members of the group were Ginger Spice, Sporty Spice, Scary Spice, Baby Spice and Posh Spice

But while it is permissible to omit the comma between the last two items, writers have a choice to put one in if they want to – and if they do, the extra comma is termed an Oxford comma. So in this sentence, the comma after *Portugal* is an Oxford comma:

> The semi-finalists were France, Germany, Portugal, and Wales

With this example, the comma does not really help the reader, who already knows that the semi-finals must involve four teams. But in other cases, the position is less clear:

> Waiting staff should ask the wedding guests to choose two of the following to accompany their main course: green salad, coleslaw, seasonal vegetables and new potatoes.

Here, the absence of the comma leads to an ambiguity: do guests have a choice of two out of four possibilities, or do 'seasonal vegetables and new potatoes' represent a single choice so that there is only a choice of two from three? If the writer means to signify four, the Oxford comma can avoid confusion:

> Waiting staff should ask the wedding guests to choose two of the following to accompany their main course: green salad, coleslaw, seasonal vegetables, and new potatoes.

Some writers favour always using the Oxford comma to avoid ambiguities of this sort, or the momentary confusion caused to a reader unfamiliar with the legal market who reads:

> The student had fixed up vacation schemes with Shepherd and Wedderburn, Allen & Overy and Slaughter and May (how many firms is that?)

Restrictive and non-restrictive clauses: the comma as important signifier

Here are two sentences, identical except for the commas:

The associate who had drafted the contract then circulated it to the other side for comments

The associate, who had drafted the contract, then circulated it to the other side for comments

Readers get a different sense of the significance of *who had drafted the contract* from these two sentences.

The first, without the commas, is read as what grammarians call **restrictively**. The words *who had drafted the contract* serve to identify the associate who circulated the contract, answering perhaps the question *Who was it who circulated the contract to the other side for comments?* You can't leave the words *who had drafted the contract* out without robbing the sentence of its main meaning. Some people call a clause like *who had drafted the contract* in a sentence like this an **identifying** or a **defining** clause.

The second sentence, with the commas, is read **non-restrictively**. The reader is assumed to have a particular associate in mind, and the phrase about drafting the contract serves to give some extra information about him or her – here, that he or she had drafted the contract. The question answered might be: *What did the associate do next, and why?* If the words were omitted, the main meaning of the sentence would be intact.

Here, then is a case where a convention about punctuation actually alters the meaning the reader gleans from the words in a sentence. The point is especially marked when the subject is a person and the relative pronoun is therefore *who* – as in the case above.

More about restrictive and non-restrictive clauses: which *and* that

When the subject isn't a person, the commas are not the only marker of difference between a restrictive and non-restrictive use. The difference is also marked, by many careful writers, by choosing *that* (with no commas) where the restrictive use is intended, but *which* (with commas) where extra information is being imparted

> The university ***that*** came top in the survey was awarded £5m of extra funding by the Department (restrictive: identifies the university in question from among a group)

> The university, ***which*** came top in the survey, was awarded £5m of extra funding by the Department (non-restrictive: we already know which university the writer is referring to, and *which came top in the survey* tells us more about it)

But the *which/that* rule is by no means universally obeyed. Though not many writers would use *that* in a non-restrictive sentence, it is common to see *which* used in a restrictive sentence. The reader is left to infer, from the absence of commas, that the words are used with a restrictive force:

> The university which came top in the survey was awarded £5m of extra funding by the Department

Readers naturally take *which came top in the survey* to be restrictive, identifying the university that was awarded the funding. It follows that the commas – or absence of them – is seen as a stronger indicator of the restrictive/non-restrictive boundary than is the choice of *that* or *which*.

Careful writers should always obey the 'comma or no comma' convention.

Additionally, while they're unlikely to be seriously criticised if they don't, they will earn the admiration of some sophisticated readers if they are also careful to observe the distinction between *that* and *which* outlined above.

Semicolons and colons

It's possible to do without these marks, and it may be safer to do so if you can't remember which one to use. But the rules for using them are not that hard, and just occasionally, they can if used accurately achieve an effect that you can't otherwise produce.

The most common problem writers have with semicolons and colons is working out when to use which. The differences are explained below.

The semicolon (;)

We have already seen that a semicolon is one solution to the dreaded 'comma splice'. In this use it is quite close to a full stop – which is itself another way of eliminating the comma splice. The semicolon, when used like this, separates what would otherwise be full sentences.

To this you might retort: short sentences are usually easier for reader to follow. Isn't it therefore always better to use full stops rather than semicolons?

The answer to this is: yes, shorter sentences are usually better. But sometimes, a writer may want to suggest that ideas are more interconnected than separate sentences would imply. It often appears where a contrast is drawn – compare:

> The bookmakers consistently predicted a win for Remain. The polls were more equivocal, and sometimes showed Leave ahead

> The bookmakers consistently predicted a win for Remain; the polls were more equivocal, and sometimes showed Leave ahead

The antithesis is slightly more clearly marked in the version with the semicolon.

And – unlike, as we shall see, with a colon – the two parts of a sentence falling either side of the semicolon need not bear any particular relationship to one another:

> The thunderstorm had abated several hours before; the school secretary opened the gates to the playing field

Because the semicolon marks an intermediate level of interruption between a comma and a full stop, it can also be useful where commas occur within the components of a sentence:

> The flags were red, white and blue; the sun shone, hazily but warmly, on the square; and the mayor, accompanied by two or three gendarmes, walked stiffly towards the war memorial

or simply to provide a stronger skeleton for a sentence of over average length, like this one from earlier in the guide:

> Going for *she* and *her* consistently instead seems equally discriminatory; alternating between *he* and *him* on the one hand, and *she* and *her* on the other, in successive chapters artificial and confusing; using *he/she* (or *(s)he*) and *him/her* merely laborious

The colon (:)

A colon fulfils a slightly different function from a semicolon, marking the relationship of the two parts of the sentence.

Generally, the part of the sentence that follows the colon amplifies, exemplifies or explains the part that precedes it. For example:

> The onset of the disease is characterised by distressing symptoms: patients may suffer nausea, severe headaches or even hallucinations

> Nobody should underestimate the impact of the floods: more than twelve thousand people remain homeless after two months

> Two entirely different types of blunder occur regularly in contract drafting: modifiers are used indiscriminately, or one part of the drafting simply contradicts another

It helps to imagine the colon as a point around which the sentence **pivots**.

A semicolon, by contrast, separates parts of a sentence that operate **in parallel** to one another.

A colon also introduces a list:

> Several players have won the men's singles at Wimbledon only once: Agassi, Stich and Hewitt are examples

In contract drafting, a colon is used to introduce separate sub-paragraphs, and semicolons to separate them:

> The Company shall send a copy of any Enforcement Notice it receives to:
>
> a) the Seller;
>
> b) the Seller's auditors; and
>
> c) the Prudential Regulation Authority
>
> within 7 days of receiving it

Capital letters

Capital letters used to be common in mid-sentence – here is John Donne in the 1620s:

> The ashes of an **Oak**, in the **Chimney**, are no epitaph of that **Oak**, to tell me how high or how large that was…

But in modern English writing (particularly in Britain), capital letters in midsentence are less favoured.

Lawyers generally overuse capital letters, and thus reinforce the profession's reputation for old-fashioned writing. Bryan Garner, a noted US legal language commentator, says fairly that in legal writing 'there is an unfortunate tendency towards contagious capitalization'.

Some brief guidance is given below.

Don't, in an email of advice, use capitals for ordinary English words:

> The **Company** will have to disclose its remuneration policy to its **Regulator**

unless, exceptionally, you are using terms in a specialised way which the reader will readily understand (for example, you are discussing the obligations arising under a contract in which the capitalised terms *Company* and *Regulator* are defined terms).

Be hesitant before using in email writing the contract technique of defining terms (using capital initial letters for the definition). It comes across as overformal, and it is usually clear enough from the context which *company* or *regulator* (say) you are referring to.

Don't use (including in a contract) a capital letter after a colon or semicolon, neither of which marks a new sentence.

Don't WRITE IN ALL CAPITALS. You sometime see this in contract drafting, and it comes across as shouty and inconsiderate to readers.

Do use a capital 'I' for the first person pronoun. Lapses into lower case 'i' belong only in informal communications between friends, not professional writing.

In contracts, use capitalised terms only when the expression is separately defined in a definitions schedule or within the relevant clause. If a capitalised term is defined, use it consistently.

Distinguish between parts of a title (capitalised) and mere descriptions:

> *Professor Bottletop* is a *professor* at *Bristol University*. *Bristol University* is a *university* with a prominent reputation in the study of law

> I visited *Death Valley*, and also the *valley* of the *Mississippi*

> The *central Australian* climate is very different from that of *Central America*

The phrase an *Act of Parliament* has capital letters. A named bill conventionally has capitals but a simple reference to a bill does not, so:

> The *Finance Bill* is a *bill* which annually foreshadows a corresponding *Finance Act*

Do not capitalise seasons unless they are, as they are in the title of the poem in this example but not in the reference to when it was published, personifications:

> Keats' Ode to *Autumn* was published in the *summer* of 1820

Some names are inconsistent, and the correct usage just has to be learned case by case:

> The capital of *the Netherlands* is *The Hague*

Capitalised letters are used when words come from proper nouns:

> Larry was the *Prince Charming* of the postroom

He's the Prince Charming of the post room

unless the connection has faded:

> They **boycotted** the demonstration, and ate a **sandwich** in front of the **rugby** instead (the connection with the originals – Captain Boycott, the Earl of Sandwich and Rugby School – is no longer vivid in people's minds).

Some adjectives can appear in both capitalised and lower case forms, depending on the context:

> They enjoyed a **platonic** relationship

but

> She studied **Platonic** ideas in the second term of her philosophy degree

Hyphens

The hyphen was stigmatised as 'the pest of the punctuation family' by Sophie Hadida in 1942. Churchill called them 'a blemish, to be avoided wherever possible'.

Usage changes. In the first two chapters of Jane Austen's *Northanger Abbey*, you come across: *rose-bush, music-master, farm-house, ball-room* and *gentle-woman*, none of which would naturally be hyphenated today. Modern practice is to suppress hyphens, so some of the above examples would in all likelihood be a single compound word (*rosebush, farmhouse, ballroom* and *gentlewoman*) and the other (*music master*) two separate words.

Some phrases are hyphenated when they are used adjectivally, but not otherwise:

> The records are not ***up to date***, and we need ***up-to-date*** records

Phrasal verbs (like *break in*, *send off* and *walk out*), which do not need a hyphen when used as verbs, do when they are used as nouns:

> The burglar tried to ***break in***

but

> We suffered a ***break-in***

Compound adjectives are often hyphenated, particularly if either of the components is an adverb or adjective:

> It was a ***well-written*** contract

> She was something of a ***good-time*** girl

But where the compound is formed of two nouns, the hyphen is often omitted:

> She is a director both of a ***steel rod manufacturer*** and of a ***pharmaceutical goods company***

Within words, sometimes a hyphen is used to avoid confusing sequences of vowels:

> When a teenager I often had a *lie-in*

or a doubling-up of consonants:

> The basement has been *damp-proofed* by a builder working *part-time*

There are some exceptions, so *cooperate* and *coordinate* are usually hyphen-free, as sometimes are *preempt* and *reelect* (though you often see the hyphenated forms instead).

A writer should obey the cardinal rule: be considerate to your reader. If there is the slightest risk of being misunderstood, even if only momentarily, and a hyphen would make things clear, use it:

> They followed a *long-travelled* path

> The blacksmith made a *spur-of-the-minute* decision

> A *man-eating* shark was photographed here last week

SHE WAS SOMETHING OF GOOD TIME GIRL

WHEN A TEENAGER I OFTEN HAD A LIE IN

THEY FOLLOWED A LONG TRAVELLED PATH

A MAN EATING SHARK WAS SPOTTED HERE LAST WEEK

Brackets and quotation marks

There's no need to spend too much time on these, but a couple of issues are worth mentioning – and illustrating – here.

Everyone knows that brackets come in pairs, but it can be difficult to decide how they fit in with other punctuation. The simple rule to remember is that where the brackets enclose a whole sentence, they also enclose the full stop that closes that sentence. (The full stop is, of course, itself part of the sentence.)

But where the brackets only enclose **part** of a sentence, the full stop goes outside the bracket (even where the bracketed words are the last words in the sentence).

Good writers use brackets sparingly, since they tend to make writing indigestibly stodgy. Most lawyers overuse brackets when they write.

A similar issue arises with quotation marks (sometimes called 'quotes'). Here there is a difference between US and British practice which goes beyond whether to use 'single quotes', more common in British English, or the "double quotes" often preferred by US writers.

Here's the question that most often crops up: when the quoted material ends a sentence, do you put the full stop before or after the quotation marks?

British style is to follow the same rule as with brackets explained above. In other words, the quotes are placed outside the full stop if what is quoted is a full sentence:

> Her first thought was: 'I ought to set off before seven o'clock, in case the ticket office is shut by the time I get to the station.'

But if what is quoted is merely a fragment of a sentence, the quotes precede the full stop:

> She caught the train anyway, which had been delayed by 'the wrong kind of leaves on the line'.

US writers prefer to put the full stop inside the quotes in both cases.

A few commonly confused or misspelt words

This guide is not intended as a dictionary. But it may be helpful to record one or two cases where lawyers sometimes fail to distinguish between two words with closely similar meanings, or which sound very much like one another but mean different things. A reader may be surprised at, and think the less of, a lawyer who gets the words wrong.

Advice/advise

The verb form is with the 's':

I'd **advise** you do the following

The noun has the 'c':

That's my **advice**

US writers agree (there's no difference between British and American uses as there is with *licence/license* and *practice/practise*: see below).

Complement/compliment

A *complement* is that which makes something complete:

The advertising campaign involved a series of TV commercials, **complemented** by a leaflet drop

A *compliment* is a praising remark, and *complimentary* has extended its sense to something like 'gratuitous'. So when a restaurant offers its diners a chocolate at the end of a meal, it is *complimentary* (free) but only by a stretch *complementary* – it's not really needed to make the meal complete, but is just a gratuitous add-on.

Council/counsel

A *council* is a group of people meeting together for a particular purpose, such as the *Council of Trent* or *Wandsworth Borough Council*. If I give you advice, I *counsel* you (verb), or give you *counsel* (noun). A barrister is often referred to as *counsel* or *Counsel*. *Counsel* is not a word that readily appears in the plural: all my advice together may be wise *counsel* but is not wise *counsels*; the QC and junior barristers on a case are together *counsel*, not *counsels*. A *counsellor*, in Britain, is someone who gives advice on a specific area, such as marriage problems or bereavement, whereas a *councillor* is someone with a seat on a *council*.

Dependant/dependent/independent

A *dependant* (noun) relies on another for support, on whom he or she is *dependent* (adjective). A self-reliant person is *independent*.

In the US, it's *Independence* Day, not *Independance* Day, on 4 July – there is no such word as *independant* or *independance*.

Imminent/immanent

If an event is soon to happen, it's *imminent*. *Immanent* means something different – pervasive (usually of a non-material quality). So for example:

> The inhabitants believed the divine spirit to be **immanent** in all living things

Judgment/judgement

The version with the 'e' is more commonly used to denote the quality of wise discernment, and the version without the 'e' often used to denote the oral or written determination by a judge deciding a case. There is in reality no difference between these alternatives, either of which is correct, but writers may as well observe the distinction to avoid being looked down on unfairly by those who think there is a real difference.

Lead/led

The past tense of *lead* is *led* (it is not like *read*, whose past tense form retains the 'a').

Liaise

Liaise has two 'i's, not one. It is a backformation from the French. Furthermore, though the word is less often encountered in a legal context, the noun is *liaison*, not *liason*.

Licence/license

Here – as with *practice/practise* below - there is a difference between British and US usage. In British usage, the noun form is *licence*, and the verb form *license*, so James Bond has a *licence* to kill but his films are *licensed* for distribution. In the US, *license* is used for both forms, so what a British driver calls a driving *licence* is in the US a driver's *license*.

Mitigate/militate

To *mitigate* is to soften or make less harsh, so a plea in *mitigation* is one that is submitted in the hope of sparing the accused harsh punishment. To *militate* is to strive or contend, so the youth of an offender may *militate* against (weigh against) harsh punishment and the judge may decide to *mitigate* the sentence.

Negotiate

Not *negociate*, which is tempting for those familiar with the French language, in which a *négociant* is a merchant.

Oral/verbal

These two are often confused, to the irritation of readers who know and respect the distinction. *Oral* means by the mouth, so (in most legal contexts) delivered in speech rather than in writing. *Verbal* simply means in words. So an email or text is an example of *verbal* communication. The error you most often see is committed by those who think that *verbal* signifies *oral*, so you see, erroneously:

> the contract was **verbal** only – it had not been reduced to writing

Practice/practise

These two words differ as between British and US usage.

In Britain, a solicitor *practises* (verb) law, and often works in a solicitors' *practice* (noun). In the US, to *practice* is a verb also.

Prescribe/proscribe

To *prescribe* is to impose or recommend – hence, a doctor issues a *prescription* for the medication a patient is advised to take. To *proscribe* is to ban or forbid.